Sadie Hasler

Pramkicker

T0286375

Bloomsbury Methuen Drama
An imprint of Bloomsbury Publishing Plc

B L O O M S B U R Y
LONDON • OXFORD • NEW YORK • NEW DELHI • SYDNEY

Bloomsbury Methuen Drama

An imprint of Bloomsbury Publishing Plc

Imprint previously known as Methuen Drama

50 Bedford Square	1385 Broadway
London	New York
WC1B 3DP	NY 10018
UK	USA

www.bloomsbury.com

**BLOOMSBURY, METHUEN DRAMA and the Diana logo
are trademarks of Bloomsbury Publishing Plc**

First published 2016

British Library Cataloguing-in-Publication Data
A catalogue record for this book is available from the British Library.

ISBN: PB: 978-1-4742-9253-5
ePDF: 978-1-4742-9252-8
ePub: 978-1-4742-9251-1

Library of Congress Cataloging-in-Publication Data
A catalog record for this book is available from the Library of Congress

Series: Modern Plays

Cover design: Olivia D'Cruz

Typeset by Mark Heslington Ltd, Scarborough, North Yorkshire
Printed and bound in Great Britain

Pramkicker

Pramkicker

PREVIOUS OLD TRUNK

PREVIOUS SOLO

Sadie Hasler

Sadie Hasler is co-Artistic Director, playwright and actor of theatre company Old Trunk. She is also a multi award-winning columnist, and has written and performed extensively in television, radio and on the international comedy circuit. Her one woman show *Lady Bones*, bastardised biographies of famous dead women, opened in Melbourne in 2010 before running at the Pleasance Edinburgh and touring the UK to critical acclaim. She is currently editing her first novel.

In addition to writing for performance, Sadie writes regularly for publications. She has been the Society of Editors' Regional Columnist of the Year and EDF Media Awards' Regional Columnist of the Year. She was commissioned to write a piece on suicide and grief for *The Lancet*, is a core contributor and collective member for new alternative women's magazine *Standard Issue*, set up by Sarah Millican, and writes weekly for *The Southend/Basildon/Canvey Echos* and *The Colchester Gazette*.

"Lovely" – **Matt Haig**

"Wonderful" – **Sarah Millican**

"Excellent...a perspective that mental health journals don't cover enough. It is an honour to print this." – **Editor, The Lancet**

"I can't begin to explain how brilliant Sadie Hasler is. Her journalism and fictional writing is utterly exceptional. Breathtaking." – **Phill Jupitus**

After the *Pramkicker* tour, Hasler will be playing Leni in her new play *Fran & Leni*, a play written for the fortieth anniversary of punk which will premiere at Latitude Festival 2016 and go on to Assembly for the Edinburgh Fringe.

Sarah Mayhew

Sarah Mayhew is an actor, improviser and former dancer. She started her career touring the world with renowned Circo Tihany. She regularly performed on the London circuit as part of the successful Joan Crawford Collective, and produced and starred in improv troupe Quirkish Delight for twelve years.

Before playing Jude in *Pramkicker*, Sarah starred in numerous other plays by Hasler: as Beatrice in T*he Bastard Children of Remington Steele* which garnered 4- and 5-star reviews and was named pick of the Edinburgh fringe, as Enid in *The Secret Wives of Andy Williams*, and as Ted Hughes, Bette Davis, Emily Brontë and Rose West in a version of *Lady Bones*, adapted for two women for a national tour. Sarah will be playing Fran in Old Trunk's forthcoming production *Fran & Leni*.

About Old Trunk

Old Trunk was born in bed, by text. Sadie huffed, "I just want to do plays all the time", and Sarah said "OK". The name came a few minutes later when Sadie's eyes fell on her father's old boarding school trunk. Four years later, Old Trunk has grown to become a tireless two-girl operation, fuelled by feist, love and black coffee – dedicated to creating strong roles for women, in plays which are driven by women, which seeth and emote.

Old Trunk are proud of the biography they have built thusfar.

Their first play *The Bastard Children of Remington Steele* premiered at Camden People's Theatre, went on to a week's run at the Leicester Square Theatre, and then appeared to critical acclaim on alternate days with its prequel *The Secret Wives of Andy Williams* at Underbelly for the Edinburgh Fringe 2014.

They went on to present a scratch performance of play-in-development, *Blazed*, at Pulse Festival 2015.

Pramkicker premiered at the Marlborough Theatre, Brighton in May 2015, went on to Latitude Festival, Assembly for Edinburgh Fringe 2015, then was invited to be part of the King's Head Theatre's forty-year anniversary celebration of new writing.

In addition to their main productions, Old Trunk were featured in an *Observer* spread as pick of the Fringe, appeared at the Storytellers Club at Latitude 2014, appeared in *The Sunday Times Magazine* as a company "making waves", were selected for the prestigious Escalator East To Edinburgh scheme in 2014, curated the Old Trunk theatre tent for Metal's Village Green Festival 2013, represented the Arts at the House of Commons, run the successful storytelling night Tales & Ales, showcasing new work by acclaimed authors, scriptwriters, poets and performers, and toured *Lady Bones* round the UK.

After the *Pramkicker* tour, Old Trunk will be premiering their new work *Fran & Leni* at Latitude Festival 2016 before running at Assembly for the Edinburgh Fringe.

They are indebted to the love and support of wonderful patrons Deborah Frances-White, Phill Jupitus, and Jenny Eclair, and are supremely grateful to Arts Council England for seeing something worth supporting, having been awarded funding four times, most recently for the research and development, and subsequently tour of *Pramkicker*. They would never have considered certain possibilities were it not for the mentorship from wonderful arts organization Metal Southend and Anthony Roberts of Colchester Arts Centre.

Pramkicker will be touring to the following in 2016:

Colchester Arts Centre – 4th May

London, King's Head Theatre – 10th–15th May

Margate, Tom Thumb Theatre – 21st May

Brighton, Marlborough Theatre – 3rd–4th June

Southend, Clifftown Theatre – 7th June

Norwich Arts Centre – 8th June

Oxford Playhouse – 23rd June

Manchester, Waterside Theatre – 1st July

Chelmsford, Fling Festival – 2nd July

Peterborough, Key Theatre – 7th July

Hornchurch, Queen's Theatre – 19th September

For my life wench, the best person to write plays for.

Boundless thanks and love for very many things go to:

Deborah Frances-White for being Deborah Frances-White, Phillip
Jupitus for all the Joopsing, Jenny Eclair for generally existing,
Sarah Millican for she knows what, Benjy Adams for being our rock
of calm, Andy Delaney for being a fucking genius, Charlie Platt for
being our loyal Ginge, our Edward Mitchell who we miss a lot,
Matthew Boulter for being calm and kind through doubt and mess,
Marc Mollica for his beautiful brain, Fi and Dave Dulake and their
stellar hub of art the Railway Hotel, Colette Bailey and Sean
McLoughlin and all at Metal Southend, Paul Watson and Drew
Aspland at the old Alex, the incomparable Anthony Roberts and
Andy Winmill at Colchester Arts Centre, clever boys Oliver Johnson
and James Bergerson at Rescape, Jack Bence for coming to play,
Chris Erskine at Seedbed for his astounding generosity, the
wonderful gang at Assembly Edinburgh, Tess and all at Clifftown
Theatre, the high priestess of art and minxiness Tania Harrison for
everything and the tireless, big-hearted supporter Jonquil Coy.

Dan Nixon and Conrad Williams at Blake Friedmann for being all-
round acebombs, Arts Council England for seeing something to
support.

Particular thanks go to our darling girl, producer extraordinaire
Sarah Georgeson for sending my manuscript off without my fucking
permission, and the excellently clever John O'Donovan at
Bloomsbury Methuen Drama for coming with his apple and not
thinking the play was shit.

Endless thanks must also go to the wonderful people who donated
to our Pramkicker Kickstarter fund. You guys are all swaddled in the
trunk of love.

Deborah Francis-White, Daddy Warbucks, Susan Calman, Richard
Herring, Jonquil Coy, Milly Thomas, Vinay Patel, Tania Harrison,
Mickey Noonan, Susie Boniface, Mathew Lyons, Adrian Tyte, Susan
Turnbull, Maggie and Andrew Dennis, Laura Hasler, Sam Hensey,
Matthew Boulter, Isabel and Graham Boulter, Jean and Ivor Dennis,
Corinne Taylor, Veronica Over, Becky Connor, Amy Fox, Virginia

Loveridge, Charlie Platt, Edward Mitchell, Andy Winmill, Fi Dulake, Judy Nylon, Palmar Jack Perkin, Dan Trelfer, Robbie Knox, Harriet Carmichael, Mandy Crandale, Debbie Crandale, Sarah Kim Beck, Drew Aspland, Paul Schiernecker, Ben Mudd, Ian Bourne, Dave Collins, Ian Pile, Owen Williams, Ben Hickman, Joanna McLoughlin, David Woodcock, Malcolm Hunt, Russell Hughes, Carrie Marx, Ricky Champ, Lindsay Lucas-Bartlett, Julie Seal, Claire Eastham, Jay Laker, Jason Stone, Shelley Mills, Gabriel Vogt, Pope Lonergan, Jo Farrugia, Robert Carlisle, Wendy Solomon, Kate Cooper, Lizzie Jones Stables, Michelle Bamber, Diana Collier, Becky Brown, Mark Lancaster, Neale Fraser, Paul Bappoo, Beth Harrison, Sophie Skillett, Gina Decio, Peter Finlay, Rachel Keys, Sandie McQuaid, Lucy Julian, Emily Barrand, Sanjay Patel, Nikki Nicholas, Lesley Butcher, Charles Sharman-Cox, Sue Johnson, Jen Puddick, Michelle Bappoo, Steve Berry, Keira Lyons, Anonymous, Tim Stokes, Jane Scoggins, Joanna Rutherford, Paddy Fairhead, Lesley Brian, Asuvini Ratnamaheson, Kate Crudgington, Katie McEwan, Kirsty Smith, Alison Zatta, Lynn Delderfield, Alex Mowatt, Matthew Elmes, Steve Chapman, Adam Booker, James Gawman, Rachel Stoneley, Lee Tearrell, Chris Noons, Luke Mason, Gavin Kerruish, Tina Parnham, Pip Hazell, Yasmeen Skelton, Hannah O'Rourke, Guy Douglas, Barbara Platt, Simon Uskuri and Jenni Bray.

Pramkicker premiered at the Marlborough Theatre, Brighton in May 2015 with the following cast:

Jude   Sarah Mayhew
Susie   Sadie Hasler

Writer   Sadie Hasler
Director   Sarah Mayhew
Assistant Producer   Sarah Georgeson
Sound and Light Designer and Operator   Benjy Adams

Pramkicker

Joan Jett's 'Bad Reputation'. Music cuts at 'I don't give a damn about my reputation'. Lights up. **Jude** *and* **Susie** *are sat, looking at the audience, who are 'the group'. It is Session 1 of* **Jude**'s *anger management course. She is seething with impatience.* **Susie** *tries her best to explain things cordially when* **Jude** *is too volatile to try.*

Jude   Let's get this over with shall we. I had a slight situation and now they think I'm mental.

Susie   She kicked a pram.

Jude   I kicked a fucking pram.

Susie   It fell down some steps. That seems to be the thing that's causing most of the . . . *consternation.*

Jude   A little stairway. Hardly a mountain.

Susie   And . . . it did rip a fire extinguisher off the wall, causing some damage to the plasterwork . . . and a canvas of Hepburn to go on the . . . wonk.

Jude   Audrey. Not Katharine. Obviously.

Susie   Nobody puts Katharine on a canvas. She's too sassy for the mass market. Androgynous. Not enough eyeliner. Wore trousers.

Jude   Don't get me started.

Susie   Well, this is sort of the right place. You might as well let it out.

Jude   This is Suse, my sister, by the way.

Susie *waves and smiles.*

Jude   She's just here . . . why are you here again, Suse?

Susie *blinks. She's forgotten what she's meant to say.*

Susie   Oh. Yeah. I've got the rage really bad too. I could go at any moment. Danger.

Jude   Yeah right.

Susie   Also, damage limitation. *She* can be a bit . . . (*Makes 'danger' eyes.*)

Jude   Anyway. The 'mother', the owner of the pram, the pass-ag bitch, said she'll let it 'drop' if I get 'anger management', which is hilarious because she was the one doing all the screaming.

Susie (*chuckles*)   She did do a bit of screaming.

Jude   So here I am.

Quick flick to the coffee shop. **Susie** *becomes* **Amber**, *the 'pass-ag bitch', kneeling on the floor with her assortment of invisible children.*

Jude   Sorry, can I just get through? Sorry, no, I just want to get to the . . . I just need to get to . . .

Amber (*charmingly*)   Jasper, come to Mummy. Jasper, come to Mummy now, come on . . . (*Suddenly losing it.*) TILLY! STOP DOING THAT TO MILLY'S HEAD. MILLY, STOP DOING THAT TO TILLY'S HEAD! JASPER! RIGHT, ALL OF YOU STOP EVERYTHING NOW! (*Noticing* **Jude** *trying to get past her.*) Sorry, could you just move? Thanks.

Jude   What?

Amber   Yes, sorry, just . . . could you . . . move? You're getting very close to the children's artwork there.

Jude   I'm getting a coffee. This is where you get the coffee from. And you and your fucking art gallery are sort of . . . blocking *that*.

Amber   Well. Costa has more space. You might be happier there.

Jude   Costa's extra space is filled with double the prams, double the kids, and double the mothers wilfully ignoring them. Maybe *you'd* be happier there.

Amber   Oh, I don't do Costa. I only like independent coffee emporiums.

Jude EMPORIUMS? Look. That's fine, love. Be 'independent', but you don't have to block the way for other 'independent' people who just want to come in for a coffee. Can't you leave the prams chained up outside or something? Get a bike lock? Leave the kids at home? In the bath? Something?

Amber Oh. I get it.

Beat.

Could you not have babies?

Jude Excuse me?

Amber Bless you. It must be so hard, validating your existence.

Jude WHAT?

Amber (*laying her hand on* **Jude***'s shoulder, who looks like she might explode*) Bless you.

Jude (*throwing* **Amber***'s hand aside, to the group*) Bless me? FUCKING BLESS ME? She squeezed out that fat Nutella-encrusted little arsehole

Susie – Slash lovely baby –

Jude – into a tepid paddling pool, just about kept her minge from falling out, probably mildly aware that in all her drugless pushing she'd done an unsightly little turd – the vision of which, along with her gaping baby wound, her husband will never be able to unsee.

Susie *becomes* **Amber** *again momentarily.*

Amber (*to audience*) I did . . . *soil* myself when I had Jasper. I did. I think it was all the months of love and worry coming out? You know? Also, I'd had a lot of organic pineapple. I was an absolute slut for it.

Jude And she's blessing me?! Bless yourself, love! Bless you! *I've* never shat myself in a pool! And I just *lost* it.

Susie (*to herself*)   Argh.

Jude   I was just so fucking angry. They're fucking everywhere with their fucking massive prams and their fucking abysmally behaved children and their fucking sense of self-righteous fucking gift to the fucking world –

Susie   We're allowed to swear, right?

Jude   And she pushed me.

Susie   Coz we swear a bit.

Jude   So I kicked the pram.

Susie   Hard.

Jude   And the pram went flying.

Susie   Fucking fast.

Jude   And the front wheels went over the step.

Susie   Uh oh.

Jude   And that was that.

Susie   And it fell down the stairs – bam bam bam.

Jude   . . . Yeah.

Susie   Into the street.

She trails off, wide-eyed. Pause. Then, as if it makes it better . . .

The kid wasn't in it.

Jude   Oh Christ no, the kid wasn't in it, I'm not *mental*. The *kid* was banging a fucking xylophone in Creativity Corner with his equally horrendous little friend –

Susie   Maximillian, rocking the dungarees by the way.

Jude   – and was blissfully fucking unaware of the whole 'your mother's an arsehole' situation.

Susie   We thought the Creativity Corner might inspire us.

Jude   But it was for kids, OBVIOUSLY.

Susie (*quite excited*)   They had a speak and spell.

Jude *gives her a withering look.*

Susie   What? I never had one.

Jude (*rolling her eyes*)   Those fucking prams are a trip hazard, I don't know how they get away with them. I think there was milk on the floor too, I almost slipped coming in.

Susie (*dryly*)   Probably breast milk.

Jude   Maybe it *was* breast milk.

Susie   OH MY GOD, I WAS JOKING.

Jude   No, seriously, Suse! Maybe I could sue.

Her eyes widen at the thought.

If we could trace the DNA back to her actual tit it might turn out that it was all her fault anyway! *The pram slipped on the essence of its source of its need to exist.* Now that, Susie, is fucking Schroedinger.

Susie   No, Jude. That is fucking not. That's something you've completely made up. And they've probably mopped since then.

Jude   I thought I felt a twinge this morning. That – was whiplash.

Susie   OK, I think claiming whiplash after you're the one that kicked off is pushing it.

Jude   Kicked off is a bit strong.

Susie   It's not though, is it.

Jude   It wasn't that bad. It could have been worse.

Susie   Yes, but you didn't just kick the pram though did you?

Pause.

Jude   No.

Susie   There was *the other stuff*, wasn't there?

Jude   There was some . . . other stuff, yes.

Susie   Which was . . . ?

Jude   OK, I *may* have got her in a headlock BUT SHE CAME AT ME FIRST.

Susie *has become* **Amber** *again, is up on her feet, and re-enacts the patronising hand-clap on* **Jude**'s *shoulder.*

Amber   Bless you.

Jude *slaps her hand away and turns to go.* **Amber** *holds her wrist as if hurt, and slaps* **Jude**'s *shoulder like a catty schoolgirl.* **Jude** *turns like a tigress and flicks* **Amber**'s *tit.* **Amber** *flicks her tit back.* **Jude** *then punches* **Amber**'s *tit.* **Amber** *punches* **Jude**'s *tit back. They part, holding their tits in pain, and begin prowling around each other, hissing, making strange animal noises.* **Amber** *slowly approaches* **Jude** *and proclaims:*

Amber   You will die alone.

Jude   Yeah? Well your kids are fuck ugly.

Amber   You *bitch*.

Amber *grabs* **Jude**'s *neck and pulls her in for a sort of awkward rotating tussle, biting her arm.*

Jude   Ow. Do not bite me. Do not bite me. I said – DO. NOT. BITE. ME.

Jude *grabs* **Amber**, *forcibly removes her, spins her, and hurls her across the room.* **Amber** *lands facedown on the beanbags in Creativity Corner.* **Jude** *hurls herself on top of her, legs astride.*

Jude   And I *may* have taken her down in Creativity Corner but that Cath Kidston covered, Babyccino-buying, olive-gobbling twit BIT ME!

The felled **Amber** *becomes a squished and dishevelled* **Susie**.

Susie   You do know I'm not her right?!

Jude   Ugh. Yes. (*Gets up.*) I let her go.

Susie   Yeah, eventually. When the barista grabbed your wrists and told you he knew jujitsu.

Jude (*scoffs*)   That queen? Pilates, MAX. OK. I admit I may have gone a bit far when I smeared jam all over her face. But in my defence (*Proudly.*) it was organic.

Susie *turns to audience as* **Amber**, *happy to divulge her maternal secrets.*

Amber   I don't give my babies anything that hasn't ripened naturally in the sun? I like to think of it as the sun working its way down into their little tummies? It's the least I can do for Jasper, Tilly, Milly and Montgomery.

She's gone again.

Jude   And I may have said to Montgomery that he better get used to seeing his momma pushed down like the ho she is. I went urban. I have no idea why.

Susie   They had a Banksy on the wall? Maybe it was that?

Jude   Yes! Right. So, no, it wasn't *just* the kicking of the pram. It was some other stuff. But I stand by it.

Susie   Jude, you're supposed to be sorry or she will press charges.

Jude   Right. I don't stand *by* it, as such, but those are my reasons and my reasons are their own thing and I can't be held accountable for those, especially when those reasons only came about because of a stuck-up middle-class get-my-paps-out in Pizza Express twit!

Susie (*to the group*)   She really is very sorry.

Jude   Yes. Can I go now? Have I managed my anger enough for you guys? Is this how it works?

V/O – **Janet**, *the counsellor, finally speaks.*

Janet   Jude, I think you definitely have some things to work through. I think these sessions could be good for you, and as PC Lyons said, if you don't show a bit more contrition, you're . . .

Jude   Fucked.

Janet   Well, yes. Fucked.

Jude   Fine. (*Slowly, sarcastically.*) I'm sorry.

Janet   Don't treat me like a cunt, Jude. I may be wearing a blouse and provide the biscuits out of my own pocket, but I'm not a moron and this isn't school – you can't sate me with bullshit. I've got five degrees. And an iguana. See you next week.

Jude *and* **Susie** *are stunned.*

Jude   Woah.

Susie   C bomb.

Jude   Unprofessional.

Susie   Iguana?

Jude   Did not see *that*.

Susie   Drink?

Jude   What's stronger than gin?

Susie   . . . Five gins?

Jude   That.

They high-five. Joan Jett bursts out again as the girls flop down into their beanbags. They are now in their lounge, several drinks later.

Jude   I'll tell you what I can't stand about all those fucking mothers.

Expectant pause.

Susie   Go on.

Jude   The way there's just no fucking *thought* going on. It's like they were programmed from birth, with all those dolls that piss and cry. And everything is SHITTING PINK.

Susie   We do need some mothers you know.

Jude   Hmm. Theoretically. Ours was pretty shit though, wasn't she?

Susie   Jude!

Jude   She was though, wasn't she? Perfectly nice, but ineffectual.

Susie (*thinks. Then, reluctantly*)   Yes.

Jude   I never really get why they had kids, other than it's just 'what you do'. I always knew they'd fuck off abroad. They prefer it when it's just the two of them.

Susie   That's why I always wanted to hang around with you.

Jude   Yeah, you little tagalong.

Susie   I'm sorry. It must have been annoying.

Jude   It was alright. You were quite a cute kid. For a kid.

Susie *smiles at the rare compliment.*

Susie   What were you like? As a kid?

Jude   Well Suse, I . . . was a little shit. (*They laugh gleefully.*) I lived to make Mum and Dad squirm. They wanted a perfect little lady so the only toys I got given were dolls. Fucking dolls. So I used to rip off their heads and arms and legs and bury them in the garden. When Mum asked me what I'd done with them I said they'd gone to Mexico. I was obsessed with Mexico. Oh my god. They're probably all still out there in the mud, poor fuckers. Right, one day, in the summer, when it's nice we are going to get pissed and rip up the garden.

Susie   Er. Jude. Did you never go in the potting shed?

Jude   Only to smoke. And get fingered by Dean Lobley. Badly. Twice. Why?

Susie   Coz they were all in there. The doll's heads. I found them one day, dug them all up. Dad was digging up the flowerbeds when he was going through his courgette and potato phase and they were everywhere. I mean obviously I thought they were tiny mermaids from the pond who'd crawled through the earth in search of a prince and had their heads cut off by worms. Then I realised.

Jude (*proud*)   Me.

Susie (*smiles*)   You. Dad was fucking furious! Chucked them in the compost. I snuck them out, dusted them off, and hid them in the potting shed. They were like my treasure. I put some in shoebox beds. Some in empty plant pots. Hung some of the limbs from garden twine in case fairies needed leg transplants. I gave my favourite ones spanners for bodies and put them in dad's toolbox. But they got claustrophobic so I put them in a banana crate coz there's loads more room. And then they were really happy and had discos and stuff.

Jude *is stunned.*

Jude   You pissed all over my precociously brilliant artistic feminist statement?

Susie   Yeah.

Jude   Fuck you. You're cute.

Susie   Thanks. Sorry. Backyard Tracy Emin.

Jude   S'alright, Little Miss Frankenfreak.

Pause. **Susie** *finally acknowledges the ambient music that has been playing.*

Susie   Jude, what *is* this music?

Jude   Brian Eno. It was on the list they gave me of helpful peaceful shit that might stop me killing people one day. Wank isn't it?

Susie   I kind of like it. It's like floating in the womb.

Jude   You are a hippy.

Susie   And you are a cunt.

Jude   Top marks for an unexpected C bomb.

Susie   I learned from the best. Night.

Jude *smiles as* **Susie** *leaves.*

Anger Management Session 2

V/O **Janet**   Right, in this session I think it's important for you to take ownership over your own behaviour. And the course. Right. I'll be in . . . my office. Email me if there's any problems. Don't break anything; I will charge double.

Jude (*on her phone*)   Susie – where are the frick are you? Don't leave me with these freaks.

Susie *comes bustling in.*

Susie   Hey.

Jude   Oh. (*Into phone.*) Bye-by-by-by-bye. (*Hangs up.*)

Susie   Sorry. Had to pop to Boots before it shut. Where's whatsername?

Jude   Janet? Oh yeah. She said hi on Skype and fucked off. Again. Probably taking her iguana to the Bodleian Library.

There is an awkward silence as no one talks. **Jude** *and* **Susie** *stare at each other awkwardly.* **Jude** *can't bear it anymore.*

Jude   Oh for fuck's sake. Anyone got any anger they want to talk about? I think I more than did my bit last week. Got anything you can jazz this shit up with? Any old anger in the closet? Any bodies?

Susie *becomes meek middle-class* **Belinda***, in with the audience.*

Belinda   Erm. I've got some things I'd like to say?

Jude   Great. What's your name, love?

Belinda   Belinda.

Jude   Off you go, Belinda. And try and make this glorified biscuit club worth an hour of my life.

Belinda   Erm. Well, I just wanted to say. I don't really think I suffer with anger as such? It's just my husband occasionally finds me, you know, throwing things around the kitchen and says it's anger problems? But it's not so much anger, it's just what I feel like when, when he's . . . *at home. S*o I thought I'd try and get a bit of it out there and see what that's about rather than, you know, *kill him.* But that wouldn't be anger as such, if I did, that would just be because he's a GIANT BASTARD.

Stunned silence.

Jude (*slow clap*)   Woah. Thanks, Belinda.

Belinda (*laughing gently with relief*)   Well, that was very helpful, thank you. Right. I'd better get going. I've got to get the tea on before Malcolm gets back. Thank you.

Pause.

Jude   Jees-us. Mad as a bowl of tits. OK. Anyone else or are we done?

Susie *has exited as* **Belinda***, and now becomes* **TJ***, booming in gangster London patois from the back.* **Jude** *becomes quite prim.*

TJ   Hey, yo. Pramkickah.

Jude   Excuse me?

TJ   Pramkickah.

Jude   Do you mean me?

TJ   Dat's whattisaid . . .

Jude   Yes?

TJ   Why'd you kick dat pram anyways, dough?

Jude   Because I was verbally assaulted by a socially reprehensible scraggy-titted bitch with bad highlights.

TJ   She sounds fit. Yeeah, nah though, but there's always like dicks being dicks everywhere all the time and you don't always go round kickin deir shit. You must have been loaded and ready to blow already. Whyyy?

Jude (*astounded*)   Well. That is none of your business.

TJ   Pffffffffff. Fair enough. But it is sort of why we's here.

Jude   Well. You raise a good point. And perhaps one day I shall tell you. Come on, Susie. We're done here. Pub.

Susie *comes forward and smiles at the group. She tries to think of a helpful goodbye.*

Susie   Just . . . take it easy, yeah guys?

Jude   Susie! PUB!

Susie   Alright!

They are in the pub, sipping in silence. **Susie** *has been waiting for the right moment.* **Jude** *is expecting it.*

Susie   So?

Jude   So what?

Susie   Why did you kick the pram, really?

Jude   I knew that was coming.

Susie   Yeah. I can't believe I haven't asked already. I can't believe I bought that it was just some mum 'annoying' you.

Jude   She belittled my life in front of a café full of shitty-nappy-toting vacuous twits. Is that not enough?

Susie   No. Not to get her in a headlock and kick her fucking pram, no. There's loads of mums like that around; you've never lost it before. Tell me. There's a good chance I'll understand, you know. Because I'm your sister, and because I'm not a fucking moron. Jude!

Gives up coaxing and slaps her knee.

Jude   Ow! OK. I was a little bit cross.

Pause.

A lot cross.

Susie *waits.*

Jude   OK. I was . . . *hurt.*

This is hard for her to confess.

Susie   Bingo. Do go on.

Jude   OK. I was heading back from the bank to meet you, headphones on so I couldn't hear '*the people*', when . . .

Jude *is in the street.* **Susie** *becomes* **Jason**, **Jude**'s *posh athletic ex.*

Jason   Jude! Judy! Hey. I thought it was you.

Jude (*gutted to have been seen*)   It's . . . me!

Jason   It's me.

Beat.

Jason.

Jude (*faux blasé*)   Oh. Hi. Yes, Jason.

Jason   How are you?

Jude   I am fantastic, thank you. (*Reluctantly.*) Are . . . you?

Jason   Yeah. Late, on my way to football, but saw you and wanted to say hi. It's been years, right?

Jude   Yeah. Hi.

Awkward pause as **Jason**'s *gaze falls to her tits.*

Jude   Are those yours?

Jason (*glancing around to see what she means*)   Oh. Yeah! My boys! Elliot and Michael. Boys! Away from the road!

Jude   Right. They're . . . big.

Jason   Yeah! Ten and eight now.

Jude   Ten and eight. *Ten?*

Jason   Oh. (*Mild panic.*) Yeah. Er. So. Molly got . . . pregnant not long after you and I . . . split.

Jude   . . . Nice.

Jason   Yeah. Wasn't planned. I assumed she was on the thing . . . But she, she wasn't. And Molly doesn't believe in getting rid. You know, got a womb, use it. All that. So . . . she . . . won me round.

Jude (*disgusted*)   Molly sounds lovely.

Jason (*looks a bit broken*)   Yeah. She's a great mum. So . . . what about you?

Jude   Oh, still in marketing. I hate it but the bonuses are great. Mum and Dad fucked off to live in the south of France so I'm officially house-sitting, essentially till they die which is sort of morbid but I'm saving shitloads on rent. They come back every Christmas. Suse, my sister . . .

Jason   I remember Susie! Great girl.

Jude   Yeah, she's just moved back for a bit too, so we hang out a lot. Getting drunk, getting to know each other really, she was always so young before. Generally living the high life, you know. Nothing's changed really. Too busy for a relationship. Might get a dog. All that really.

Jason   Cool.

Jude (*too quickly*)   Yeah. Really cool.

Jason   Well. Good to see you, Judy Rude. You're looking good.

Jude   . . . You too.

Jason   Take care, yeah?

Jason *grasps her arm in a similar motif to* **Amber**'s *'bless you'* *gesture.*

Jason *becomes* **Susie** *again, and* **Jude** *and* **Susie** *are sat once more in the pub.*

Jude   He called me by my name. His name for me. Judy Rude. Because I 'always swear'. Apparently. The only fucking person I have ever allowed to call me Judy. I went and stood in a card shop for a bit to sort my head out. I hadn't seen him since we split up, not once. Ten years. It's weird – I always thought I wasn't that bothered about him, but I've not really liked anyone since. Not enough to live with. And you don't expect that when you break up with someone do you? That they won't be bettered. Upgraded. That you will just . . . stand still. Ten years. Fuck.

So I stood there in the shop, and there were loads of congratulations cards – new babies, pink and blue, storks with bundles, balloons, all spewing out. There was one, with a photo of fat little baby feet, next to a card which said 'It's your birthday, let's get wankered'. And all of a sudden I didn't know who I was anymore. Was I free? Or wasted? Just for a minute. Then I was fine. Left the shop.

AND THEN OF COURSE I STARTED GOING FUCKING STIR-FUCKING-CRAZY THINKING OF ALL THE THINGS I COULD HAVE SAID. Like, 'What the fuck were you doing having a kid months after breaking up with me', like 'You said you were like me, you never wanted kids', like 'Damn straight I look good – I haven't been sucked dry by tit-leeches'. And then I almost threw up, because that lady who smells of egg went by, and also because what if, what if we'd stayed together, what if he'd asked me, and I'd said yes in a moment of madness and let him do his thing, and we'd done the normal stuff, and had the babies, would that be my life now? Would I be happy? Happier? Different? What? WHY WASN'T I GOOD ENOUGH TO WANT TO IMPREGNATE? How come Judy Rude lost out to Molly Blah?

Beat.

Susie   Erm. Is that an actual question?

Jude   Yes? Why not! Yes!

Susie   Well – you're a bit . . . *shouty*.

Jude   I REGRET NOTHING.

Susie   I KNOW!

Jude   I am the Edith fucking Piaf of the empty womb. Je ne regrettay fucking rien.

Susie   I know you don't, Jude. You don't have to tell me.

Jude   I know, but *he* doesn't know that I don't want to have kids, still. That I *still* don't want to have kids. He just saw someone he used to fuck, that he used to love, for seven *years* used to love, who's now ten years older (but who looks only five years older) and he judged me for not having the same thing he does.

Susie   I doubt he would have judged you for it.

Jude   He *judged*. And I wasn't even looking my most awesome. I was going to wear my new power thing, you know with the thing, but I thought I didn't want to waste it BECAUSE I WAS ONLY GOING FOR A FUCKING COFFEE WITH A LOAD OF FUCKING MOTHERS.

Susie   And me.

Jude   And you. My baby sister. How cool.

Susie   Cheers. I am thirty now, you know that, right?

Pause.

Jude   Then I was trying to get to the café to meet you and I couldn't get down the fucking street for all the fucking prams blocking the way – they were like a bloody funeral procession – and I couldn't get along quick enough, I just needed to *move*, but they were blocking me, and one of the mums just stopped dead in the middle of the fucking pavement in front of me and I had to swerve to miss bumping her arse, and the only place I could go was the road. So I stood in the *gutter*, four-by-fours packed with their two point fours going past me as I stood looking at all these women with their massive baby-carriers and their bags bursting with baby stuff and their wandering children, and I thought to myself –

'I don't count.' In the eyes of everyone else, in the grand dream scheme of society, I don't count as much as the mothers or the babies. I am the lesser creature. I probably wouldn't even make it onto the lifeboat if the ship was going down. I'd probably be left to get twatted in the boiler room with the fucking violinist. And that is when I got to the café. And I kicked the fucking pram.

Susie   Hard.

Jude   And the pram went flying.

Susie   Fast.

Jude   And the front wheels went over the step. And that was that.

Susie   And it fell down the stairs – bam bam bam.

Jude   . . . Yeah. And here we are.

Pause.

He looked at me with pity, Suse.

Susie   Did he though?

Jude   Yeah, I could see it.

Susie   Because you're childless?

Jude   CHILDFREE.

Susie (*corrects herself*)   Childfree.

Jude   Because I haven't changed.

Susie   But, that's OK. That's *good*.

Jude   NO IT'S NOT. I should have had something better to say. I want to look him up, get him to meet me and wear my thing with the thing and say 'no no no no' (*waves a sassy finger*) then leave, looking fabulous.

Susie   We could do that!

Jude   Oh, what's the point. No matter how fabulous I look and hilarious I am he's clearly into the twee family shit. Boden catalogue, Center Parcs bullshit. I'd be wasted on him. Not that I want him. I don't *want* him. I just want him to know that . . . I'm cool. That I stick by my choice.

Susie   I get it. I really do. But you need to get it out of your system and then move on.

Jude   Move on to what?

Susie   Whatever you like. That's the point, isn't it. You can do whatever you like.

Jude   Gah. Life, you prick. Gin?

Jude *and* **Susie** *exit. Tail-end burst of Joan Jett.*

Anger Management Session 3

Susie *enters alone. She smiles at the group nervously.*

Susie   Jude'll be along in a min . . . (*Looks at text message.*) Oh. No she won't. Nice one, Jude . . . I'll . . . probably just go then . . .

Susie *goes to leave.*

Dominique   Running after your big sister again, are you?

Dominique *is a woman who finds herself in anger management at the behest of her family though she sees no problem in 'just being assertive'.*

Susie   Er. No.

Dominique   God, she's got you right where she wants you, hasn't she?

Susie   Er no, she hasn't.

Dominique   Yes she has. Wow. She is one controlling bitch.

Susie (*suddenly incensed, protective of* **Jude**)   Er. EXCUSE ME, no she is not. Jesus. Rude. I happen to think she's . . . cool. She knows what she wants, likes, is, isn't, wants to be. She doesn't give a shit. I don't know fucking anything. Do you?

She falters. She's not used to being angry.

She is brilliantly bonkers though though, isn't she Belinda?

She seeks solace in the face of mad **Belinda**, *then rethinks. This is her chance to splurge.*

Susie   OK. FINE. Growing up with her was . . . *challenging*. There. Being eight years behind her was like being the tail of a bloody kite, just bouncing along behind. She was the centre of everything in my universe, it all orbited her, and I was just . . . *me*. The invisible satellite. The little sister. But I thought she was just amazing.

She taught me to swim. In the sea. Said I didn't need the baby pool because it wasn't real. She let me bob in her arms for hours at a time until I was ready to paddle off on my own.

She'd always swim out to the crowstone, then go way past it like she was trying to get to Kent, which I thought was France, like a dick. I'd try and keep up, but I couldn't. One day she kept on going and I thought that's it, she's in France and I'll never see her again. And I could see her, laughing with men in berets with loads of onions and fancy ladies in fur coats with cigarettes on sticks, and I was so scared. I kept swimming but she was nowhere; I couldn't find her. Then the waves got big, and the back of my head kept smacking hard against them as I tried to keep my chin out of the water and my mouth was filling with solid chugs of salt and I thought I was drowning. I was probably close, but I wasn't afraid of dying. I was afraid of not being with her. I called out, hoping I could make my voice carry to France. Jude! Jude! JUDY!!

Jude *appears.*

Jude   If you ever call me Judy again I will fucking kill you.

Susie *coughs feebly.*

Susie (*sheepishly*)   She'd only swum to the edge of an old dinghy and was doing pull-ups on the side. She swam us all the way back, me under one arm. She dried me off, put my shoes on, and walked with her hand on my head, all the way home. Put me in a nice warm bath.

Jude   Silly Susie Soo.

Susie   Soon after, she left home. But *that* is how I know what it feels like when Jude is on your side. Strength. Bravery. Life.

Susie *is home.* **Jude** *is drinking.*

Jude   Hi babe. Sorry about that. Shocker of a day and couldn't face it. Sorry for the late text. Were you there already?

Susie   Yeah.

Jude   Shit. Sorry.

Susie (*still moody*)   'S'alright.

Jude   Do you want gin? I got Tanqueray. You can pretend you're that bloke you like, Hemingway. You like that.

Susie   No. I don't fancy it. Thanks.

Jude   OK then. Well it's in the fridge. Next to a custard slice.

Susie (*smiles despite herself*)   Thanks.

Pause. Something is bugging her.

Jude? Where did you go when you left? Home I mean.

Jude   Here and there.

Susie   Yeah, but. Where, here and there? Where?

Jude   Mexico. Ibiza mainly. It doesn't really matter. The places don't mean anything. I just had to go.

Susie (*irritated*)   Yes, but why though?

Jude   I had an itch. For as long as I could remember. The feeling that there were things out there that had been kept from me. That Mum and Dad had been keeping the curtains closed on the world.

Susie *tuts and sits down.*

Jude   Travelled about a bit doing bar jobs and waitressing. Came back. Ended up living with some high class prostitutes in South Kensington. As you do.

Susie *is stunned.*

Susie   Obviously.

Susie *looks at* **Jude** *intently, expecting more.*

Jude   What? Oh my god, do you want my life history?

Susie   Yes, yes I fucking do, Jude! You never tell me anything!

Jude   Fine. Well. I worked at French Connection in the day, folding, folding, hanging, folding, and in the evening I took my classes at Pineapple. I'd fucking dance for hours – spin, stretch, drop, spin, till I almost broke myself – I just wanted to sweat it all out. And at night I sort of collapsed. Drank. Picked up the phone for the girls. Marcy Minneapolis, took no shit. Yenka, mad Russian. I think they taught me that I wasn't really strong. Not really. Those girls were fucking steel. They made everything look so easy, but refined. I even tried it once.

Susie *blinks.* **Jude**, *nods, sheepish.*

Jude   I was bored working in the shop, wondered . . . what it was like. How easy it would be. They had a guy who came round from time to time. He brought them coke, their dealer I guess, though he didn't dress or act like one, wannabe yuppy, hung around hinting for blow jobs he never got. I never saw them pay him – these girls really knew how to get stuff. He must have thought it would be coming his way, one day. I'd gotten myself a bit hooked on their gear, and I drank their champagne like it was fucking juice so was permanently off my tits, and I didn't know what harm it could do if it was for coke and not money, you know? If he gave me money it would have felt cheap, but coke? Ha. That wasn't *payment*. That was *swapping*. Ha. I was so fucked.

And one night he was just . . . *there*.

Susie *appears behind* **Jude** *and becomes him –* **Gordon**. *She caresses* **Jude**'s *tit from behind, strokes her hair. She smiles.*

Jude   We ended up messing around a bit and I thought I could do it, but by the time I realised I couldn't (**Gordon** *pulls her head back roughly by the hair and pulls her down to the floor.*) he wasn't listening – the music was pretty loud – maybe he couldn't hear me when I tried to stop him . . .

Gordon *smacks her head down on the floor then pulls it up again by the hair, squeezes her mouth with one hand.*

Gordon   Yeah. Got used to the good stuff didn't you, you greedy girl. That's it – fucking bend over and show me how much you like it, you lovely little cunt.

He smashes her down again.

Jude *stays down, face against the floor, arse in the air.* **Gordon** *becomes* **Susie**. *She sits down, stunned, horrified.*

Jude   I couldn't move, I was too fucked, but I could hear my voice shouting no, in my head – couldn't he hear me. And there I was spread out on the coffee table with the blow everywhere, my arms stuck under me, the thick of his palm pushing my neck down, my hair caught in his fingers, his other hand flicking, everywhere, over me, yanking my clothes, undoing himself, creeping in, forcing . . . and I felt myself go from shock to . . . numb. His rhythm was shit. Like a drummer with one stick. He seemed annoyed with himself, with me. I realised how weak he was.

Jude *is suddenly furious.*

He was a fucking idiot. My eyes cleared like I'd plunged into water and something rushed up in me. And I lamped him. With the champagne bottle. I'd been keeping my eyes on the words Moet et Chandon the whole fucking time. He didn't pass out but his nose burst open. Blood pissed over the carpet. And I panicked more about that because it was really fucking expensive fluffy white shit. He rushed out telling me he'd report us all but I knew he never would, not with what we knew about him. I don't really know if it . . . was . . . (*The R word is silent.*) Even now. Lots don't do they. But I know I tried to stop it. I did.

She nods sadly at **Susie** *who is teetering on tears.*

Jude   So.

She shrugs.

The girls came in, cleared up, didn't say a word, didn't need to. Marcy ran me a bath. Yenka poured me a drink – vodka, naturally.

Susie *stands up as* **Yenka**, *a no-nonsense hot Russian.*

Yenka   You drink. Is good for you. Is the potatoes. (*Beat.*) And the booze.

Jude   And fixed me with the strangest look (**Yenka** *takes* **Jude**'s *chin in her hand and surveys her face.*) I have ever got from another woman. I can still see her. It was like she was saying . . .

Yenka   Shit got real huh, lyublmaya? You're woman now.

Yenka *pushes* **Jude***'s face away with a flick of her thumb, turns, sits, and is* **Susie** *again, aghast.*

Jude   I worried for a bit. Waited for my period. I don't think he finished, but there's always that first bit isn't there. The thin bit. Be just my luck. When I saw blood in my pants I cried. They call it your friend sometimes don't they. And it is. The girls got a nicer dealer named Leroy, gay as they come, and it was all aceballs again. For a bit. Then I left. I had to. I was fucked all the time. Got the sack from my job. Used to sleep all day, and at night I would walk round the park. And I felt . . . so *lonely*. I knew something had to change. Because this wasn't who I was. So I came home. I had just enough money for the train. The moment I saw the sea from the window I knew I'd be alright. And I was.

Pause.

Susie (*quietly, just about keeping it together*)   Fuck.

Jude   Yeah. Fuck. (*She laughs feebly.*) Another life.

Susie   Thank you for telling me.

Jude   Think differently of your big sis now?

Susie   Yes. But not bad. Good.

Jude   Good.

Susie   Jude, was that why? Is all *that* why you don't want kids?

Jude   God. No! I mean, I can sort of see why you'd think that, but no. I just always knew, Suse. Some women just know. I was fifteen when I realised. That was before . . . everything . . . and I just really *knew* I didn't have the feelings you need. Maybe it's nature. Or anti-nature. Oh I don't know cos I'm no good at science.

She laughs.

Susie (*the tears come back*)   I'm so sorry.

Jude   Why are you sorry, silly?

Susie   About him, doing that to you.

She nearly breaks.

Jude   Oh. Ha. (*Pause.*) His name was . . . *Gordon*. Has there ever been a good Gordon?

Susie (*thinks*)   The gin dude?

Jude   Well that fucks that then.

They both laugh, relieved to be laughing.

Susie   Better than getting fucked by a Beefeater I guess.

Jude (*faux-doubtful*)   I dunno.

Susie   They probably leave their hats on, dirty bastards. It'd be like the queen was watching and wanking from the shadows.

Jude   Every now and then I forget you're a sick fuck.

Susie   I am my sister's sister. (*Curtsies.*)

Jude   Ha.

Pause. She goes thoughtful again.

I remember thinking what a tiny cock he had. In amongst the mess of having my face pushed down, admittedly into some of Bolivia's finest, and thinking '*What the fuck do I do, just let this happen?*', I almost wanted to laugh. I almost wish I could relive it now so I could turn round and say 'Hey, *Gordon*, if this is rape at least make sure you're equipped to make it hurt afterwards so I know what to call it.'

Susie *is stunned.*

Susie   You're right. That would be . . . *lovely.*

Jude   Ha. You little fuck.

They laugh. **Susie** *goes to sit by* **Jude**'s *feet.*

Susie   This is nice. Being home. With you. Talking.

Jude   Thank your fuckwit ex for dumping your arse by text then.

Susie   Ouch.

Jude   Sorry. I went dark.

Susie   Yeah you fucking did, Jude. Jesus. No, well, it's good. For the best. Yay.

Pause. Something is troubling **Susie**.

Susie   Jude, do you really never wonder what it would be like, being a mum?

Jude   Yes. I do sometimes wonder. But not a lot. Not enough. I've been happy doing other things. I just don't parade those things around in a pram. Look Suse, I'm not selfish, whatever that may mean, I'm not heartless, and I don't hate children. These are the things I chose for *me*. And really – can you imagine me on a school run? Christ.

Susie   Is it enough though?

Jude   Oh for fuck's sake – is anything ever enough? Is there anyone in the world who never wonders if there could be something more for them? Look Susie, this is fine. This is *good*. OK?

Susie   OK.

Jude   Right. Enough.

Susie   OK.

Jude   We need music.

Jude *flicks through her iPhone – past Blondie, ABBA, Aretha and finds Dirty Dancing – 'I've Had The Time of My Life'. She looks gleeful.* **Susie**'s *eyes open wide in panic. She goes to crawl away.*

Jude   Remember this?

Susie   No.

Jude   Yes, you do.

Susie   No, I don't.

Jude   Come on, Suse.

Susie   No, Jude, please.

Jude   Come on, let's get our Swayze on.

Susie   Oh, for fuck's sake, Jude. Swayze's dead.

*They begin to dance, a cobbled-together bastardised little girl version
of the Dirty Dancing routine. But now, they are women.* **Jude** *leads,
obviously.* **Susie** *begins to enjoy it despite herself. It becomes joyous.
The music goes from lo-fi and tinny to a full stage blare. They are in
the film.*

Jude   You're not that bad actually. Probably coz you've been
fucked a few times now. That's all dancing is isn't it.
Substitute fucking. And freedom. But mostly fucking. Right.
We're doing the lift.

Susie *falters.*

Susie   What?

Jude   We're fucking doing it. Come on.

Susie (*panicking, begins the run up*)   Oh, for fuck's sake, Jude.
SHIT SHIT SHIT SHIT SHIT FUCK.

THE LIFT. **Susie** *is suspended in the air, it is briefly glorious, her
arms outstretch, then she drops, staggers dizzily, and can't hold it in
any longer.*

Susie   I'm pregnant.

Jude   What?

Susie *sits down and tries to get her breath.*

Susie   I'm pregnant.

Jude   Fuck off.

Susie   That was the easy bit. I might . . . keep it.

Jude   What?

Susie   I don't know if I want to get rid of it.

Jude   But. You can't keep plants alive for longer than
a week.

Susie   I know.

Jude   You'd probably leave it outside a shop.

Susie   Probably. Even so. I might give that a go.

Jude   But you always said . . .

Susie   I KNOW. But now I don't . . . know, anymore. I
don't know, Jude.

Jude   Right. Well. Fuck.

Susie   I thought I'd be desperate to get it out, but it feels
. . . different to how I thought.

Jude   Like needing a poo?

Susie   No.

Jude   Like being constipated in the cunt?

Susie   Jesus! No! Not like that. It's. Like. A bit sick and hot
in the throat. And my boobs feel like they're going to fucking
explode. But I don't mind it. I quite like it. It's like my
insides are talking to me.

Jude   Ugh.

Susie   Yeah. I knew you wouldn't . . .

Jude   . . . understand?

Susie   Yeah.

Jude   Fuck you, Susie.

Susie   You can't fucking blame me, Jude.

Silence.

Jude   Well. You have options. You could . . .

Susie   I don't think I could. I couldn't.

Jude   It's dead easy. I've known loads of girls to have it done. It's just like having a nose bleed. Marcy Minneapolis had loads of the things. It was her contraception.

Susie *stands and becomes* **Marcy**. **Marcy** *is doing yoga, the tree position, eyes closed, blissed out. A younger* **Jude** *is copying her positions next to her.*

Marcy   I have a heavenly cunt. It would be against god's plans to mess it up with childbirth. I want my cunt to always be heavenly. I don't know why any woman would give that up. It's a gift. The gift of eternal tight cunt.

Jude   Caesarian?

Marcy   Scars are for losers.

Jude   So no babies. Never.

Marcy   Nope. Just men. And money. And my beautiful beautiful cunt. Cosmo?

Marcy *is gone.* **Susie** *sits.*

Jude   I liked Marcy. But you have more soul than she had in her little finger. More soul than she had in her tiny weeny vagina even. Alright. Let's do this. Whatever you want, however you want to do it.

Susie   Really?

Jude   Contrary to popular opinion I'm not a complete arsehole. Sometimes I'm alright. Look I'm just putting it out there. I think it's pretty cool.

Susie   Don't pretend, please. You can't do it.

Jude   No, I mean it. It's cool, doing it alone.

Susie   I thought you said you were going to help me?

Jude   No, but. Well, yes. But I mean, without . . . the dad.

Susie   Oh.

Jude   I presume the dad is fuckwit by the way?

Susie   Yeah. I went to see him, to get some stuff. We got . . . talking. And accidentally . . . did it. Then he texted after to say it hadn't changed anything. He just really liked my tits in that top.

She almost breaks, then gathers herself.

He'd make an excellent father.

She half-laughs but stops instantly.

Jude   Want me to have him killed?

Susie *thinks, then shakes her head.*

Susie   I still love him, Jude. Fuck knows why, but I do. I wish I could cut it out of me. The love, I mean.

Jude   OK. Well. It will pass. The love.

Susie   I hope so.

Pause.

Jude   You realise you've totally fucked my favourite gin buddy for the next nine months?

Susie   Eight. Sorry. Je revien.

Jude   Huh?

Susie   It was the name of the boat in *Rebecca*. 'I will return'. I always loved that. Je revien.

Jude   Such a book geek.

Susie   Eight months and I'm back, alright? Covered in someone else's sick for a change. And piss. And shit.

She realises how immense it will be.

Oh shit.

Jude   Fuck.

Susie   Yeah. Fuck.

Jude *grasps her hand and smiles an 'It'll be OK.' She exits.*

Susie *is left alone with new thoughts. She crumples.*

Susie   Nice one, Susie Soo. Oh god, what a fucking mess.

To the ceiling, suddenly angry.

When does all the knowing start?!

An option presents itself.

If I don't keep it, because it's not right, because I don't know, where does all this love go? All this fierceness in my gut? The lullabies in my mouth? The constant readiness to turn she-warrior to protect a little person that doesn't even exist yet? Can that be channelled into something else? Into work, a career, other nice humans that might need it? Or does it only ever belong to a life you create yourself? Is it really only ever motherhood that lets us scale those heights – of love?

And what if I don't know that I know in time, and time – old Father Time, the ultimate head honch of the patriarchy, no woman would design a fertile life so fucked – what if he makes my mind up for me? What if one day I go to do it, and I can't? Is *this* my chance? Will it have gone?

I think I'll mother the world. I will. I will mother the fucking world. Like Oprah. But English. And poor. And white.

And what if I don't find someone I love enough to want to do this with, who loves me more than anything else, who would be a good dad? LOVE, YOU FUCK! What a shitfest of a minefield you are!

She plonks down on the beanbag, daunted by the constant clauses in the overwhelming business of life-fucking fucking Life.

Coz you've got to find him first, haven't you? Before you get to the good stuff you've got to find him! Before all the fucking and the making love, making love and fucking, and fucking and fucking, and moving in and paying bills, and shopping and fucking, and walking and maybe cycling (coz I really want to get a bike, and he should get one too), and talking and laughing and fucking and holding hands and being sad and scared and being soul mates and cooking and eating and laughing and fighting and laughing and dreaming, and waving some dreams go past, and growing old, and growing old, and growing old. And hopefully still fucking.

And if you get even a tiny portion of all this stuff right, and nature bestows such luck, such fortune, such wham-bam thank you ma'am grace upon you – biological alchemy – all the magic of the Big Bang silently going on in that tiniest part of you, a little spermatozoa headbutting its way into an egg too small to see by the naked eye, a spark that would rattle the fucking cosmos if we could only knew the exact moment it was happening – a nice post-coital cuppa tea and the ding of the conception bell would've been fucking nice – the alakazam, the 'YOU HAVE CREATED LIFE – YOU ARE SMALL BUT MIGHTY GODS' – and then – if gestation is *kind*, and you then have . . . *a baby*, then what?

Then you've got to try and fucking get that right! A whole new person! Raise them and not break them or hurt them or taint them with our own weaknesses. And you're supposed to get that little person right without ever feeling like you've sorted yourself out to a satisfactory standard first. LIFE, YOU PRICK!

She breaks and hurls the beanbag across the stage. Her voice catches.

I want that. I do. I think. I do. I just want the love first. I *want that,* first. And then I think I'll know. And I need to know.

Susie *steps forward to a hospital counter.*

Susie   Hi, I've got an appointment for 9:15? Susan White. Yeah, sorry, I'm a bit late. A lot late. OK. Thank you.

Susie *is home.* **Jude** *comes in.*

Jude   Ahh. Where've you been?

Susie   Hospital.

Jude *looks up sharply.*

Jude   What?

Susie   Yeah.

She tries to say it brightly.

So, I'm not pregnant anymore.

Jude   What?

Susie   Yeah. My choice.

Jude   What? Why the fuck didn't you tell me?

Susie   Coz I just wanted to do it on my own. I didn't want you. For once in my life, Jude, I didn't want you.

Jude (*hurt*)   Oh. OK. Well, I understand I'd be the shit option to go to for any of that stuff.

Susie   Oh, don't pretend you're fucking offended, Jude. There's no fucking way. Just like a nosebleed, right? Easy come, easy go, all out now, all better. You've got your fucking gin buddy back now so the world can just move on without looking back, just like Jude. Not thinking, not feeling anything, just a double G and T, bit of bluster, and fuck you all.

Jude   Susie, where the fuck did this come from?

Susie (*letting rip*)   Coz I'm not ready, Jude! Am I? At all. I'd be rubbish.

She is close to tears.

And *if* I want to do it, I don't want to do it on my own.

Jude   You wouldn't *have* to do it on your own.

Susie   Or with my big sister with everyone thinking we're a fucking lesbian couple.

Jude   We'd be great lesbians.

Susie   NOT TOGETHER! We might be able to vote and abort babies but there are still some restrictions you know. You sick fuck.

They break into half-smiles and look away.

Jude   Was it OK?

Susie   No.

Her face falls.

It was fucking horrible.

She crumples and falls into **Jude***'s arms.*

Susie   And I'm effectively wearing a bloody nappy and it's chaffing and the irony is so ridiculous I could puke.

She buries her face in **Jude***'s neck.*

Jude   You're home now, Susie Soo.

Susie (*pulling away*)   You haven't called me that for years.

Jude   Just popped out.

Susie   I like it.

Jude   I can be quite the charmer.

Jude *smooths* **Susie***'s hair and lifts her face to meet hers.*

Jude   IS IT TIME FOR GIN NOW?

Susie   I don't even want gin. I just want custard.

Jude   You and your fucking custard. Fine. I'll get you custard.

She turns to go, then turns back.

Suse? I actually think you'd be a really good mum.

Pause.

Susie   Now you fucking tell me.

Beat.

Maybe one day.

Jude   Just wanted to say, in case I forget another day.

Susie   Thank you.

She watches **Jude** *go.*

Susie   Can it be tinned Ambrosia and not the powdery stuff, please.

Jude   Course.

Pause. Comes back in.

Suse. I will be there, if it happens, you know. And I'll even love it. But if you turn into one of those sanctimonious oblivious arseholes with a four-by-four pram and get in the way of my morning coffee I can't promise I won't call you a cunt, but . . . I can promise I probably won't kick you.

She stalks out.

Susie (*smiling after her*)   Deal.

Some time later. **Jude** *and* **Susie** *are in the garden.* **Susie** *is basking.* **Jude** *is staring around, industrious.*

Suse   Oh my god. It's so gorgeous. It's like summer.

Jude   Lovely day to fuck up a garden. Do we even have a spade?

Susie   Try the shed.

Jude   I fucking love a bit of gardening, me. Never done it but I sense an affinity.

Suse   You're Mother fucking Nature, babe.

Jude   Let's completely annihilate all the green shit with decking and rattan furniture.

Suse   Ooh – and lanterns!

Jude   Fine. You can have *one* lantern but we are not turning it into a fairy fucking grotto.

Suse   Fine! Don't even want one. It's not like I want it to be all Magic Faraway Tree or anything . . . I'm thirty-one. I just want somewhere to lie and get skin cancer with a margarita.

Jude *comes out of the shed holding an armful of tool-dolls. Barbie's head is on a fly-swat, a Tiny Tears head is taped to a loo-plunger, She-Ra's tied to a badminton racquet, and a Mexican souvenir doll is tied to another.*

Jude   Er. Babe?

Suse (*eyes closed to the sun*)   Yeah?

Jude   These freaky dolls of ours. Pretty much just . . . heads on tools, right?

Susie   Pretty much.

Jude   Well, if these ain't your creations then I don't know what is.

Susie *opens her eyes, beholds her old treasure, and jumps up squealing.*

Susie   Oh, my god, Jude! You fucking found them! Judy Nylon, Charlie Cow, Gingey-poo, Benjy-boo, Teddy Le Pip! SHE-RA!

She stops. She has seen her favourite. She takes it lovingly and whispers:

Chiquitita.

Jude   You are *such* a freakchild.

Susie   And you have no imagination.

Jude (*walking off*)   Fuck you.

Susie *steels herself.*

Susie   Pramkicking Prick.

Jude *laughs and takes the bait. She reapproaches slowly.*

Jude . . . . .Babykiller.

It hurts but it's funny.

Susie   Cock-biting dry-vadged old twat.

Jude (*laughs*)   Woah, you little . . .

Both   CUNT.

Susie   JINX! HA HA!

Jude   Oh my god, you jinxed me! You remember such weird shit.

Susie   I remember everything. EVERYTHING, motherfucker. I remember you pouring glue in my shoes, I remember you sewing me into my sleeping bag, I remember you rolling me up in my tent. I remember you plaiting my hair, teaching me to swim, bringing me biscuits when I was poorly, but most of all I remember missing you when you left. YOU ABSOLUTE ARSE.

Jude   WOAH, let it all out Suse.

Susie   I bloody will. I might give Janet a right old earful tomorrow.

Jude   Ahhh, yes, anger management. Yeah. I'm not going.

Susie *stares at* **Jude** *as she settles into a garden chair.*

Susie   Yes, you bloody are. One more session. One! Then you can get your little form signed, shove it up Prambitch's bumhole, and then I won't lose you to the clink.

She sits in the chair beside **Jude**.

Susie   And then we can go to Mexico. Or to Battersea and get a broken dog!

They both squeal.

But not a pug. Their faces look like anuses.

She looks disgusted. Then, wide-eyed:

Or is it anii?

Susie *ponders this, alarmed she might have been getting it wrong all along.*

Jude *watches her.*

Jude   Fuck you, Susie Soo.

Susie *looks at* **Jude**.

Susie   Fuck you, Judy Rude.

It is their I love you. They smile at each other, and look up at the sun. **Susie** *goes in for their customary 'thigh slapping' schtick and catches* **Jude** *off-guard. They slap each other a few times, then* **Jude** *forcibly takes* **Susie**'*s hand, stills it.* **Susie** *looks down at their hands entwined, women, sisters. They can do this, together.* **Jude** *tips her head back to the sun.* **Susie** *looks out at the garden, then down to the doll in her arms.*

The music swells. Very slow fade on lights. Sunset. Blackout.

Printed in Great Britain
by Amazon